AUSSIE FIRES ALIVE

Written and illustrated by

Mary-Anne Byrnes

Woolley the Wombat was in danger.

He couldn't dig.

He couldn't eat.

He couldn't swallow.

He could barely breathe.

He was very sad in the

BURNT. BURNT. BURNT BUSH.

Davo the Dingo was in danger.

He couldn't hunt.

He couldn't eat.

He couldn't swallow.

He could barely breathe.

He was badly injured by the bushfires, you see.

He was very sad in the
BURNT. BURNT. BURNT BUSH.

Tony the Turtle was in danger.

He couldn't swim.

He couldn't eat.

He couldn't swallow.

He could barely breathe.

He was badly injured by the bushfires, you see.

HE WAS IN TROUBLE.

He was very sad in the

BURNT. BURNT. BURNT BUSH.

Edward the Emu was in danger.
He couldn't run.
He couldn't eat.
He couldn't swallow.
He could barely breathe.

He was badly injured by the bushfires, you see.
HE WAS IN TROUBLE.

The ground beneath him was black.
He was very sad in the
BURNT. BURNT. BURNT BUSH.

Kenny the Kangaroo was in danger.
He couldn't hop.
He couldn't eat.
He couldn't swallow.
He could barely breathe.

He was badly injured by the bushfires, you see.
HE WAS IN TROUBLE.

The ground beneath him was black.
HOT ASH ALIVE!
He was very sad in the
BURNT. BURNT. BURNT BUSH.

Paul the Possum was in danger.

He couldn't climb.

He couldn't eat.

He couldn't swallow.

He could barely breathe.

He was badly injured by the bushfires, you see.

HE WAS IN TROUBLE.

The ground beneath him was black.

HOT ASH ALIVE!

Ash fell from the sky.

He was very sad in the

BURNT. BURNT. BURNT BUSH.

I am Kurt the Koala, and I am in danger.
I couldn't climb.
I couldn't eat.
I couldn't swallow.
I could barely breathe.
I was all alone.
I was badly injured by the bushfires, you see.

I WAS IN TROUBLE.

The ground beneath me was black.

HOT ASH ALIVE!

Ash fell from the sky. I could cry.
I was very sad in the
BURNT. BURNT. BURNT BUSH.

Not a gum leaf in sight.
Not a tree I could climb.

I sat curled up in a ball on the black, hot soil floor.

I waited, waited, and waited till death knocked on my door.

Time stood very still.
I took one last breath.

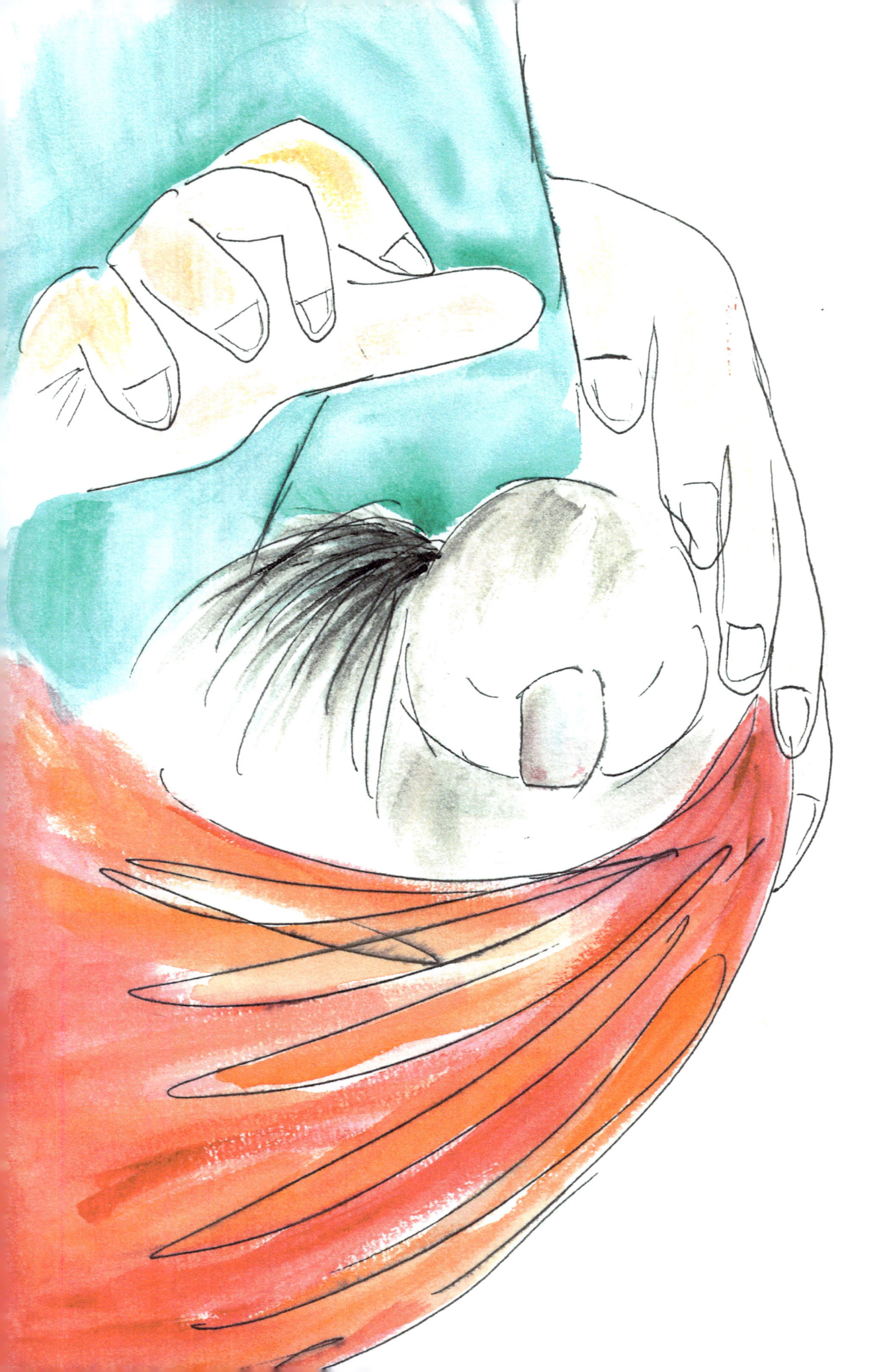

All glimmer of hope was gone till
a kind young man came along.
He carefully crouched down and
whispered a gentle song:

"We will get through this, little mate.
Hang in there.
Take a small sip of water.
Don't despair.
That's all that matters.
I care."

He bent down on one knee.
He bundled me up in a blanket, you see.

He took me to the local makeshift wildlife hospital for wounded animals.

My claws I cannot bend.
I'm on the mend.

Time will tell if and when Kurt
the Koala sees his mates again,
especially Paul the Possum.

He can't wait to see the bush blossom.
He can't wait to see it flower.
He can't wait to see it grow.
He can't wait to roam.
ROAM. ROAM. ROAM!

The Australian bush he loves to call home.
HOME. HOME. HOME!

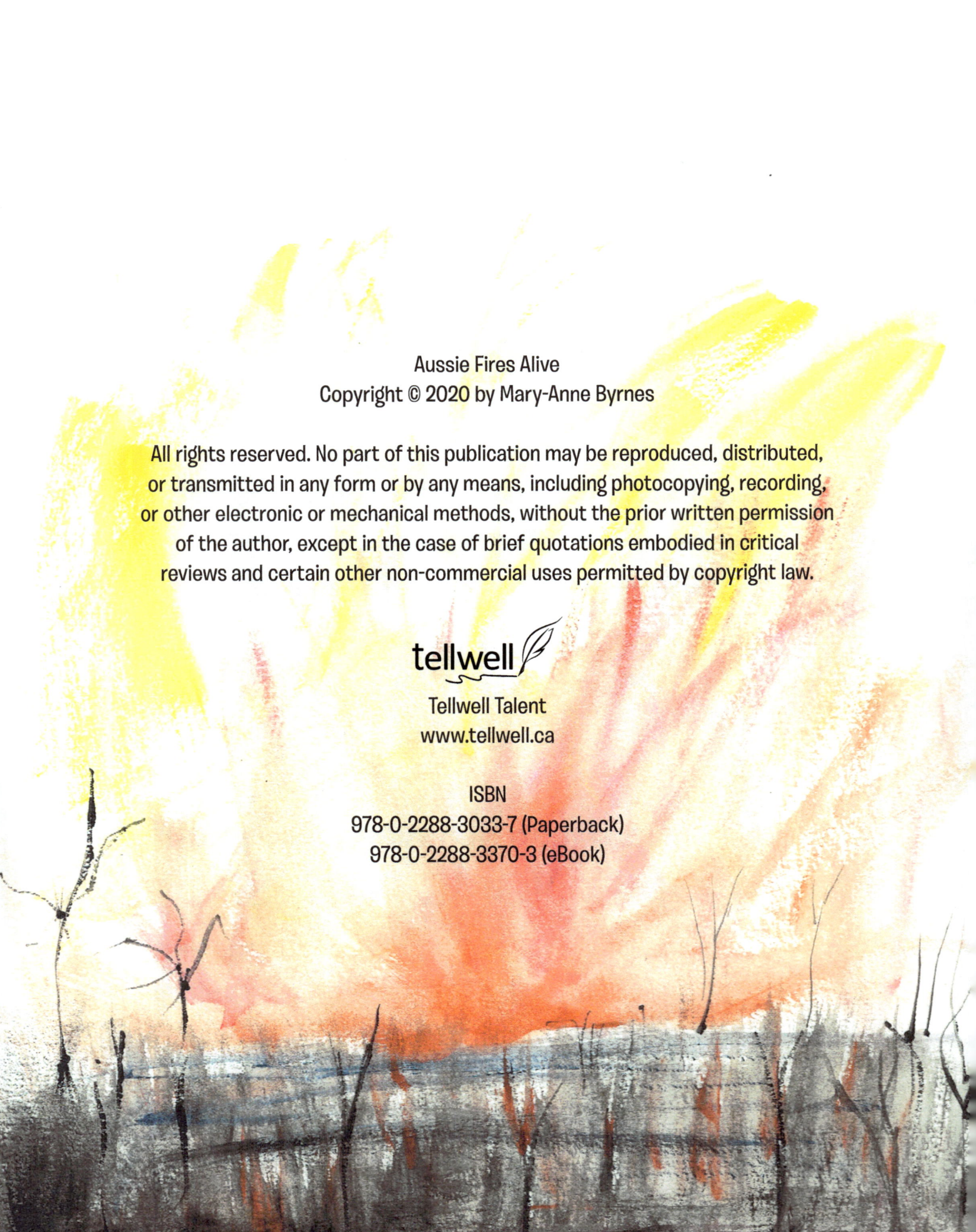

Aussie Fires Alive
Copyright © 2020 by Mary-Anne Byrnes

All rights reserved. No part of this publication may be reproduced, distributed, or transmitted in any form or by any means, including photocopying, recording, or other electronic or mechanical methods, without the prior written permission of the author, except in the case of brief quotations embodied in critical reviews and certain other non-commercial uses permitted by copyright law.

tellwell

Tellwell Talent
www.tellwell.ca

ISBN
978-0-2288-3033-7 (Paperback)
978-0-2288-3370-3 (eBook)

www.ingramcontent.com/pod-product-compliance
Lightning Source LLC
LaVergne TN
LVHW071654060526
838200LV00029B/457